The Pueblo

by Petra Press

Content Adviser: Professor Sherry L. Field,
Department of Social Science Education, College of Education,
The University of Georgia

Reading Adviser: Dr. Linda D. Labbo,
Department of Reading Education, College of Education,
The University of Georgia

COMPASS POINT BOOKS

Minneapolis, Minnesota

Compass Point Books
3722 West 50th Street, #115
Minneapolis, MN 55410

Visit Compass Point Books on the Internet at *www.compasspointbooks.com* or e-mail your request
to *custserv@compasspointbooks.com*

Photographs ©: John Elk III, cover, 8, 19, 38; Unicorn Stock Photos/E. Burciaga, 4; Kent
and Donna Dannen, 5, 7, 9, 18, 26, 30, 40; XNR Productions, Inc., 6; Marilyn
"Angel" Wynn, 10, 13, 21, 23, 32, 39; North Wind Picture Archives, 11, 12, 17, 25; Stephen
Trimble, 14; Stock Montage/The Newberry Library, 16, 29; Unicorn Stock Photos/Martin R.
Jones, 20; Photo Network/Michael Philip Manheim, 22; Hulton Getty/Archive Photos, 24; Rick
Doyle/Corbis, 27; Archive Photos, 31; Stock Montage, 33; Denver Public Library/Western History
Collection, 34, 35; Miguel Gandert/Corbis; Stephen Trimble, 37; Reuters/Jim Bourg/Archive
Photos, 41; Bettmann/Corbis, 42; Chuck Place, 43.

Editors: E. Russell Primm, Emily J. Dolbear, and Alice K. Flanagan
Photo Researcher: Svetlana Zhurkina
Photo Selector: Alice K. Flanagan
Designer: Bradfordesign, Inc.

Library of Congress Cataloging-in-Publication Data
Press, Petra.
   The Pueblo / by Petra Press.
      p. cm. — (First reports)
   Includes bibliographical references and index.
   ISBN 0-7565-0082-6 (hardcover : lib. bdg.)
   1. Pueblo Indians—History—Juvenile literature. 2. Pueblo Indians—Social life and customs—
Juvenile literature. [1. Pueblo Indians. 2. Indians of North America—Southwest, New.] I. Title.
II. Series.
   E99.P9 P739 2001
   978.9'004974—dc21   00-011282

Table of Contents

Who Are the Pueblo?

▲ *Pueblo youngsters at an intertribal dance*

The Pueblo people have lived in America for a long time. They have lived in what are now the states of Arizona, New Mexico, Colorado, and Utah for thousands of years.

Pueblo means "village" in Spanish. In the 1500s, Spanish explorers gave this name to the Pueblo people. The Spanish gave them this name because their villages looked like Spanish villages. The villages were built along a great river called the Rio Grande.

Today, there are nineteen Pueblo groups. Each group lives in its own village. Each village has its own customs.

▲ *The Pueblo have lived in Taos, New Mexico, for hundreds of years.*

▲ The original homelands of the Pueblo and their present homes.

Sixteen of the villages lie along a river in New Mexico called the Rio Grande. The Zuni, Acoma, and Laguna villages lie west of the great river. The Hopi live in Arizona. They are also part of the Pueblo family.

The Pueblo speak many languages. Some speak Tewa, Tiwa, Keresan, or Zuni. Most Pueblo also speak Spanish and English.

▲ *Acoma Pueblo*

Cliff People

▲ *Anasazi cliff houses are in the Mesa Verde National Park in Colorado.*

The Pueblo people did not always live along the Rio Grande. About A.D. 100, the Pueblo settled in what is now the Southwest. They were called the **Anasazi**, or "Ancient Ones."

▲ *The remains of Pueblo Bonito lie in Chaco Canyon.*

At first, the Anasazi lived in caves in the side of cliffs. Later, they built apartments under cliff over-hangs. Today, what is left of their villages is in Chaco Canyon in central New Mexico. These ruins are some of the most amazing in North America. Other impressive Anasazi cliff houses are in the Mesa Verde National Park in Colorado.

▲ A wall painting shows Anasazi men hunting antelope and deer.

In the beginning, the Anasazi were hunters and food gatherers. The men hunted deer and antelope in the mountains. The women gathered wild plants. Later, the Anasazi learned how to grow crops such as pumpkins, cotton, and corn, or maize.

The Anasazi lived in a desert area. They made ditches in their fields to collect rainwater and bring it to their crops. This way of bringing water to plants is called **irrigation**.

Between 1300 and 1540, the Anasazi left their villages. Some people think that a long dry spell ruined their crops. It forced the people to move south. They moved closer to the Rio Grande. The Anasazi left behind beautifully woven baskets and painted pottery.

▲ *Women ground the corn to use it for baking.*

Village Life

▲ *Inside an adobe house in Taos*

The Pueblo villages were also called pueblos. The houses were made of **adobe**—a brick of clay and straw. Today, many Pueblo families live in single-family adobe homes.

Family has always been very important to the Pueblo. Even today, families live together in groups

▲ *A modern Pueblo home in Taos*

▲ *Pueblo children belong to their mother's clan.*

called **clans**. Clans have names such as Eagle, Bear, and Antelope.

Women lead Pueblo families. They own the property and pass on their names to the children. When two people marry, they live near the wife's family. And when children are born, they are part of the mother's clan.

Each village has its own government and leaders. But all the villages work together. The people in each village farm their fields together. They grow corn, beans, squash, chili peppers, and cotton. They also raise animals.

Praying to the Spirits

▲ *The Kasha rainbow dance is one of many Pueblo religious celebrations.*

The Pueblo are very spiritual. They live in harmony with nature. They believe that spirits live in everything. They believe that spirits live in the animals, the

▲ *A special ceremony to contact the spirits*

rivers, the trees, even the rocks. Everything has a **sacred** soul that must be respected.

Pueblo priests are called **caciques**. They hold special ceremonies to reach the spirits. They ask the spirits to heal sickness, make crops grow, or protect people from danger.

▲ *The interior of a reconstructed kiva*

▲ *The corn dance is performed to help crops grow.*

At certain times of the year, the caciques honor the most important spirits, or the **kachinas**. They paint their bodies and wear carved masks. They mimic the spirits in dance and song.

▲ *A kachina*

The caciques hold some ceremonies in underground rooms called **kivas**. Only men can take part in the kiva ceremonies.

Some Pueblo artists make small wooden carvings of kachinas. They give them to the children at festival time. Other artists make kachinas to sell to tourists.

Artwork

▲ *Pueblo artists make beautiful pottery.*

Pueblo artists are known for their painted pottery. They have been making it for thousands of years. They get the clay from nearby areas. They mold it into bowls or small figures. Then they paint their creations and heat them over fire.

The Pueblo are known for their weaving too. They make beautiful

▲ *A woman weaves a yucca basket.*

baskets and clothing. The earliest Pueblo used baskets for everything from baby cradles to jars. They made their baskets out of grasses, roots, bark, and other plant materials.

Pueblo baskets were woven so tightly that they could hold water. People could also serve food and even cook in those baskets. Today, Pueblo make baskets to sell to art collectors.

By A.D. 700, the Pueblo were weaving cloth on a **loom**. Usually, women did the weaving. They used cactus and other plant fibers. They made blankets, shawls, footwear, hats, and bags out of these fibers.

Sometimes, the Pueblo women wove religious symbols and designs into the fabrics. Weaving was sacred work. The weavers were said to be weaving the Thread of Life.

▲ *A Pueblo weaving loom*

The Spanish Bring Change

▲ Spanish explorer Francisco Vasquez de Coronado and his soldiers

▲ *Catholic priests set up missions to teach their religion to the American Indians.*

In the 1500s, Spanish explorers came to what is now the American Southwest. One explorer was Francisco Vasquez de Coronado. He brought soldiers with him to look for treasures. They had heard stories about cities made of gold. They called the cities the Seven Cities of Cibola.

People from the Roman Catholic Church came with

the explorers too. They wanted the Pueblo to be Christians. They were called **missionaries**.

The Pueblo would not give up their land or their religion, however. They resisted the soldiers and the missionaries.

But the Spanish forced the Pueblo to work for them as slaves. They made them pay taxes. And they made them become Christians. People who would not become Christian or work as slaves were killed.

The lives of the Pueblo changed after the Spanish came. The Spanish soldiers killed many Pueblo. Many others died from illnesses brought by the strangers.

▲ *After the arrival of the Spanish, many Pueblo died.*

Then there was a long dry spell throughout the Southwest. The dry weather lasted more than ten years. It wiped out crops. It killed many of the cattle, sheep, and pigs the Spanish had brought.

There were other killers too. The Apache and Navajo Indians lived near the Pueblo. They often attacked Pueblo villages. They also stole what little food the Pueblo had. By 1670, many Pueblo were dying of hunger.

Fighting Back

▲ *A Hopi comes out of a kiva in this 1897 photograph.*

During this hard time, the Pueblo people turned to their religion. They celebrated their old kachina ceremonies in public. And they prayed to their gods to help them. Then, the Spanish killed some of the Pueblo priests for performing the ceremonies. They whipped others and put them in jail.

The Pueblo fought back. Leaders

▲ *The Pueblo used bricks from the ruined church in the background to build a kiva.*

from many of the villages met in secret. They made plans to drive away the Spanish. A priest named Popé became leader of the group.

In 1680, the Pueblo group killed many of the Spanish. They forced the rest of the Spanish to leave the Southwest. For the next twelve years, the Pueblo were free of Spanish rule.

Becoming Citizens

▲ *The Spanish forced the Pueblo to change their way of life.*

In 1692, Spanish troops returned to the Southwest. Two years later, Spanish were once again in control. The Spanish troops forced the Pueblo to farm the land for them. They made the Pueblo rebuild Spanish churches and ranches.

The Spanish also forced the Pueblo to fight with them against other Indian groups. The Pueblo fought with the Spanish against the Apache, the Navajo, the Ute, and the Comanche.

The Spanish ruled the Pueblo until 1821. Then Mexico won its independence from Spain. Once

▲ *Catholic churches were rebuilt after the fighting.*

▲ *A battle during the Mexican-American War*

it was a free nation, Mexico took all the Pueblo land. Mexico ruled the Pueblo until 1848.

Then the United States fought a war with Mexico and won. After that, the United States owned the land. In 1924, the Pueblo became citizens of the United States.

A New Way of Life

▲ *An early photograph of a Pueblo farmer*

When the Pueblo became U.S. citizens, they had to learn how to live in two worlds. They kept their Native American traditions. But they also lived like other Americans.

Most Pueblo could speak and write in Spanish and English. They also knew several Pueblo languages.

In the 1950s, the U.S. government encouraged the Pueblo to move into cities. But most Pueblo would not give up their farming traditions. They continued to live on the land. They became some of the best desert farmers in the world.

▲ *Fields near Taos in 1917*

Some Pueblo did move away from their villages though. Today, more and more Pueblo work outside their communities. They have jobs in factories, vineyards, and uranium mines. Many return home to their villages on the weekends.

▲ *Today, Pueblo have started new businesses, including casinos.*

How the Pueblo Live Today

▲ *A young Pueblo girl*

Today, most Pueblo live in much the same way as other Americans. The young people wear trendy clothing. They enjoy the same music, sports, and computer games as other young people do. And their parents encourage them to study hard to get into college.

At the same time, the Pueblo respect their Native

American traditions. They take part in the sacred kachina dances. They continue to make Pueblo crafts. Their kachina dolls, pottery, weaving, and jewelry are known around the world.

The Pueblo people are creating new businesses today. Many communities have built resorts, golf courses, and gambling casinos. They give tours of museums and

▲ *A Pueblo boy dressed in traditional clothing for a ceremony*

▲ A Pueblo tour guide in Taos, New Mexico

ancient places such as Chaco Canyon. These businesses provide jobs for many Pueblo. They also provide money for schools and important services for the community.

Pueblo and the Future

▲ *Cochiti Dam is one of the largest earthen dams in the United States.*

The Pueblo live in the deserts of the Southwest. Very little rain falls there. They get their water from nearby rivers and other waterways. Without these water supplies, their crops and animals would die. Tourists

▲ *Vice President Al Gore meets with members of the All-Indian Pueblo Council.*

would not visit their villages. Their popular resorts and casinos would have to close down.

For many years the Pueblo have been working together to protect their waterways. They formed a group called the All-Indian Pueblo Council. One member from each of the nineteen villages is on the council. They meet with state and local government leaders. They work to protect Pueblo waterways and sacred places.

In 1970, the Taos Pueblo won back Blue Lake. Blue Lake is a sacred Pueblo area in New Mexico. Since then, other villages have won protection for their waterways. Together, the Pueblo are building a safe future for their children.

▲ *President Richard Nixon signs the bill giving the Taos Pueblo Blue Lake.*

▲ A young Pueblo boy

Glossary

adobe—brick made of clay and straw

Anasazi—the ancient Pueblo people

caciques—Pueblo medicine men or priests

clans—groups of families

irrigation—bringing water to crops by digging ditches or canals

kachinas—the most important Pueblo spirits

kivas—underground rooms where Pueblo men take part in religious ceremonies

loom—a wooden frame on which plant fiber is woven to make clothes and rugs

missionaries—people who travel to teach religion

sacred—blessed

Did You Know?

- Pueblo children were often taken from their parents and sent to boarding schools. They were not allowed to speak their language or carry out Pueblo traditions. The federal government stopped this in 1978.

- Pueblo Americans fought bravely for the United States in World War I, World War II, Korea, Vietnam, and the Gulf War.

- A famous animal character in Pueblo folktales is a trickster named Coyote.

At a Glance

Tribal name: Pueblo

Villages: Acoma, Cochiti, Isleta, Jemez, Laguna, Nambe, Picuris, Pojoaque, Sandia, San Felipe, San Ildefonso, San Juan, Santa Ana, Santa Clara, Santo Domingo, Taos, Tesuque, Zia, Zuni

Past locations: Arizona, Colorado, New Mexico, Utah

Present locations: Arizona, New Mexico

Traditional houses: Multifamily adobe houses

Traditional clothing material: Fiber, cotton

Traditional transportation: Unknown

Traditional food: Corn, meat, wild plants

Important Dates

A.D. 100 The Pueblo (or Anasazi) settle in what is now the Southwest.

1300 The Anasazi leave their cliff apartments; the Pueblo begin settling along the Rio Grande.

1540 Francisco Vasquez de Coronado visits Pueblo villages.

1660 A ten-year dry spell begins.

1680 The Pueblo push the Spanish out of their lands.

1692 The Spanish return to the Pueblo lands.

1821 Mexico wins its independence from Spain and takes all the Pueblo land.

1848 The Mexican-American War ends; the United States gets the Pueblo land.

1924 The Pueblo become U.S. citizens.

1970 The Taos Pueblo get Blue Lake back from the U.S. government.

Want to Know More?

At the Library
Keegan, Marcia. *Pueblo Boy Growing Up in Two Worlds*. New York: Cobblehill Books, 1991.

Powell, Suzanne. *The Pueblos*. New York: Franklin Watts, 1993.

On the Web
Chetro Ketl Great Kiva
http://sipapu.ucsb.edu/kiva.html
For information about kivas

Indian Pueblo Cultural Center
http://www.indianpueblo.org/
For links to each of the nineteen Pueblo groups

Through the Mail
All-Indian Pueblo Council, Inc.
3939 San Pedro N.E., Suite E
P.O. Box 3256
Albuquerque, NM 87190-3256
To get information about the work of the nineteen Pueblo groups

On the Road
Mesa Verde National Park
P.O. Box 8
Mesa Verde National Park, CO 81330-0008
970/529-4465
To visit the impressive Anasazi cliff houses

Index

About the Author

Petra Press is a freelance writer of young adult non-fiction, specializing in the diverse culture of the Americas. Her more than twenty books include histories of U.S. immigration, education, and settlement of the West, as well as portraits of numerous indigenous cultures. She lives with her husband, David, in Milwaukee, Wisconsin.